Psychic Power

Thorsons First Directions

Psychic Power

David Lawson

Thorsons
An imprint of HarperCollins*Publishers*
77-85 Fulham Palace Road
Hammersmith, London W6 8JB

The Thorsons website address is: www.thorsons.com

Published by Thorsons in 2001

Text derived from *Principles of Psychic Potential*, published by Thorsons, 1997

10 9 8 7 6 5 4 3 2 1

Text copyright © David Lawson 2001
Copyright © HarperCollins*Publishers* 2001

Editor: Jo Kyle
Design: Wheelhouse Creative
Production: Melanie Vandevelde
Photography: PhotoDisc Europe

David Lawson asserts the moral right to be identified as author of this work

A catalogue record for this book is available from the British Library

ISBN 0 00 712357 4

Printed and bound in Hong Kong

Contents

Psychic Power

is about awakening your latent psychic abilities

for health, happiness and success

Your Psychic Potential

We all have our own unique psychic potential. We have abilities – to see, hear, feel and know – which go beyond the range of our purely physical senses of sight, hearing, touch, taste and smell. We are able to receive, access and transmit vast quantities of information, and we can learn to strengthen these abilities. Would you be surprised to hear that our intuitive and psychic senses are just as natural and normal as any of our five physical ones? Perhaps this information is new for you, or perhaps you have always instinctively felt that you have greater intuitive and sensory resources than you have yet learned to access and make use of?

We are all psychic!

Many of us are already using our psychic abilities without even knowing that we are doing it, and many more are aware of the information that they receive through their 'inner' senses but do not talk about it – often for fear that other people will not understand. Psychic potential is not something that some people have and others not; some people are just more awake to their abilities, or more naturally developed in some sensory areas, than other people. Be assured, however, that the potential is there within you and that your potential is also special and unique.

Do you sometimes think of someone two minutes before they telephone you? Do you walk into a room and pick up an atmosphere within a couple of seconds? Do you receive strong mental images or hear the answer to a question that you have inside your head before you have voiced it? Can you feel when others are upset or excited even before they speak to you or before you look in their direction to pick up the usual, physical signals? Do you have a sense that you could be able to give healing, or send thoughts to others that they will hear inside their mind? If the answer to any of these is 'yes' or even 'perhaps', this could be an indication of your unique psychic potential.

About this book

This book is concerned with awakening your psychic potential and helping you to utilize your psychic abilities for your personal development, spiritual growth, self-healing and success. In doing so, you may discover that you have abilities which you could use to help other people and support them with their development, too.

   In the following chapters we will look at some of the main areas of psychic ability: clairvoyance, auric sight, clairaudience, clairsentience, telepathy and channelling. As you read through the descriptions of these sensory areas, notice if your instincts draw you to one or two in particular. Do you already have abilities in these areas or do you have a hunch that you may be able to develop them?

The higher mind

Throughout this book you will come across the terms 'the higher mind' and 'the higher consciousness'. They refer to the concept that each of us has a part of our consciousness that acts as a bridge between the spiritual and the mental dimensions of our awareness. Simply put, we each have a reservoir of higher thought and wisdom which helps to guide the course of our lives. This part of ourselves is better able to see the bigger picture of the daily events and dramas that we become engrossed in and, if we are willing to listen to it, will enable us to put everything into perspective. Acting with the grace of our higher self can help us to make the life choices that will best support our underlying spiritual purpose and guide us in the direction of our greatest joy and

fulfilment. It is highly likely that the best decisions you have ever made began as ideas or impulses that were placed in your conscious awareness by your higher mind.

The process of actively developing your psychic potential will automatically strengthen your connection to your higher mind and allow you to work with it more effectively. The higher mind communicates to us in many ways, including sending messages to us through our psychic and intuitive senses. A certain amount of good psychic work is channelled directly from our higher consciousness which, as well as being a reservoir of wisdom in itself, acts as a bridge for information that is transmitted to us from external sources such as spirit guides and helpers.

Spirit guides and helpers

Spirit guides are personalities or energies of support that work with us to assist us in our development and the pursuit of our higher purpose. Some people choose to think of them as another aspect of their own higher mind or greater consciousness, but I tend to agree with the school of thought that considers them to be entities who are completely external to us and who communicate to us through our higher awareness and, potentially, through our psychic senses.

Spirit guides can be the source of a considerable amount of psychic information. Our own guides may communicate with us psychically to advise us about our own personal development or to support us with information for someone who is seeking our help and counsel. Other people's guides may choose to communicate through us, so that they can pass on valuable insights to the person with whom they are working. I make a number of references to spirit guides throughout this book.

Preparing Yourself to Begin

There are no absolute requirements for anyone who chooses to embark upon a journey of psychic development. The principles that I offer within this book are meant as guidelines, not hard-and-fast rules. However, it is best to begin with the right intentions. If you are developing psychically from a position of strength, this will be reflected within the success and stability of your development. Therefore, endeavour to take care of your physical wellbeing at all times.

  I would not recommend any psychic development that is linked to the use of recreational or psychedelic drugs. Anything mood-altering or hallucinogenic could potentially open your psychic senses artificially, but this kind of opening is usually damaging, unstable and ultimately limiting. If you open up your awareness naturally then you open up safely and are better able to stabilize and build upon the positive potential of your new found psychic skills. Ideally it is also best to keep alcohol, nicotine and caffeine consumption to a minimum – the majority of us function better psychically (and otherwise) when the use of these substances is minimal.

Creating the right environment

There are one or two exercises in this book which you might choose to practise with a friend or partner, and working with other people is certainly to be recommended. However, I have written most of these exercises to be primarily performed alone, in a safe, comfortable place where you are unlikely to be disturbed. Find or create a space in your home that feels warm, comfortable and secure and make it as conducive to peace and relaxation as you can. In preparing your environment you might like to follow the guidelines on *page* 12. They will prove to be helpful but, once again, they are not essential.

Exercise: Your sacred space

Once you have chosen the space that you are going to use to conduct most of your initial psychic development, take some time to cleanse it and personalize it.

1 Physically clear this area of excessive clutter and debris.
2 Spend some time cleansing and brightening the energy of this spaceby playing beautiful music, burning essential oils (jasmine, rose, lavender, neroli and frankincense are wonderful for psychic work), lighting candles, singing, chanting or visualizing this area filled with bright, healing, protective light. Do whatever feels appropriate for you.
3 Relax and meditate in this area even before you begin your exercises of psychic development. You can do this by sitting comfortably, closing your eyes and breathing deeply. To still your busy mind it may help you to focus upon the movement of your breath, in and out, and to count each exhalation.
4 Surround yourself with a few items that you find beautiful and inspirational: some flowers, perhaps, or a picture of a beautiful landscape. Choose whatever is meaningful for you.
5 When you plan to sit in this place make sure that the lighting is soft. Some people choose to meditate or do psychic work to the light of a candle, though softer electric light or gentle daylight is also fine.

Learning to relax and meditate

There are many different ways to meditate and numerous spiritual or religious traditions have their own wonderful meditation practices. At its simplest however, meditation can be divided into two categories. The first kind of meditation is concerned with engendering a level of stillness and tranquillity by giving the mind something to concentrate on that distracts it away from the thoughts and illusions of everyday life. A simple example of this is the use of the breathing technique that I have suggested in the Sacred Space Exercise opposite. The second kind of meditation is more directional, offering particular thoughts, scenarios and visualizations to stimulate specific forms of mental and emotional activity as well as engendering relaxation. Both kinds of meditation are helpful in the development of psychic potential.

The meditations in the following chapters are predominantly directional in nature. They are written for you to guide yourself through a set of ideas, concepts and visualizations that will stimulate your psychic senses. In the meditations I invite you to use some positive mental images. Some people have strong images when they do this,

some haven't. For this exercise to work for you, it is enough just to hold the idea, feeling or concept in your mind.

It would be helpful to begin each of these exercises with a couple of minutes' gentle deep breathing and a conscious decision to relax and settle your mind before proceeding. You could imagine that each thought that enters your mind turns into a beautiful bird or butterfly before flying away, leaving you feeling calm, clear and still.

Once you have calmed your thoughts a little, read through the details of the meditation exercise a couple of times to get the general idea of it, then close your eyes and relax back, trusting your mind to take you wherever you need to go. It is not essential to get every detail correct or in the right order. If you prefer, you could get a trusted friend to guide you through the meditation or you could record your own voice slowly reading it aloud so that you can use the tape to guide you.

Using daily declarations

Daily declarations are simple but powerful positive affirmations that gently help to alter your beliefs, habits and expectations from those which may be less conducive to the development of your psychic power to those which are much more so. In the chapters that follow I have included many positive declarations to aid you in developing specific psychic abilities.

  Develop a habit of using your daily declarations first thing when you wake up and last thing before you go to sleep. Keep a list of them beside your bed and do your best to memorize them for use at other times throughout the day. You can say them to yourself out loud, or repeat them silently in

your head. Alternatively, you could write them down, type them out, sing them, chant them or record yourself saying them and play yourself a tape of the declarations at regular intervals. If you are a particularly visual person, write or paint them in bright colours and paste them on to doors, mirrors, the refrigerator and other places where they will be constantly visible to you.

Here is the first set of declarations. Read it over and over to yourself, repeating them in your mind.

Declarations for safe and easy psychic development:

- It is safe for me to develop my psychic potential.

- My process of psychic awakening is easy, joyful and pleasurable.

- My psychic abilities grow in strength and stability.

- I trust myself and I trust my intuition.

- I listen to my instincts and act upon them with love and compassion.

Clairsentience

What is clairsentience?

The abilities commonly described as psychic gifts are simply natural extensions of our intuition. We have all experienced times when our intuition is acute and we are able to listen to it and respond accordingly. Your intuition tells you that it would be a good time to telephone a friend; you have a 'gut feeling' that she is in need of some support and, before you have walked across the room to pick up the telephone, it starts ringing. Your friend has beaten you to it and is telephoning you!

There are numerous examples of good choices that we make through listening effectively to our intuition. When we talk of instinct, hunches and gut feelings we are often referring to one distinct area of psychic awareness: the skills of clairsentience.

Clairsentience is particularly common, especially amongst women and children, who are still generally more emotionally-based than men. As children we are all quite open intuitively and emotionally; then, as we grow, we may learn to shut out these aspects of our awareness. Boys and men still receive messages that they have to be logical and dispassionate, and that emotional sensitivity is a bad thing. Male or female, to develop good clairsentience we need to unlearn the judgements and restrictions that were applied to us when we were growing up and become more emotionally and intuitively 'vulnerable'.

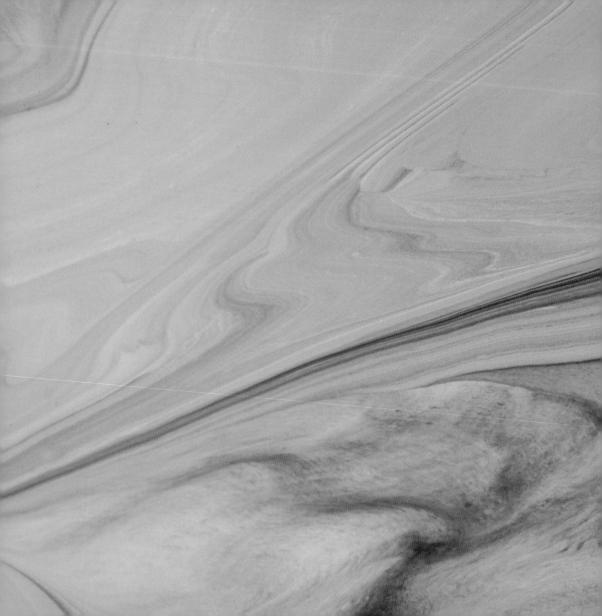

It's all in the mind!

We often dismiss our psychic abilities by telling ourselves that we are imagining things. Many of us regard our imagination as something that is unreal or illusory. A well-developed imagination however is very important for our psychic development as it provides us with an effective bridge to valuable psychic information as well as an abundance of creative energy and ability.

To develop psychically you need to give yourself permission to dream, fantasize and play before allowing your rational mind to do the necessary job of sorting, assessing and figuring out how to act upon the information that you receive.

Here are some daily declarations to help you use your imagination constructively and to open your mind, body and emotions to greater clairsentient ability. These declarations will in fact always be valuable to you regardless of your unique psychic and intuitive abilities. The development of your 'gut' awareness will always support your clairvoyant, clairaudient and healing abilities.

Daily declarations for intuitive awareness:

- It is safe for me to develop my intuition.

- My intuitive awareness grows in strength and sensitivity.

- I trust the power of my imagination.

- I easily harness and utilise my psychic gifts.

- I am a creative, imaginative, and intuitive person.

Daily declarations for clairsentience:

- It is safe for me to develop my clairsentience.

- I trust my 'gut' feelings and reactions.

- It is easy for me to act upon my clairsentient abilities.

- My instincts are valuable, effective and highly developed.

- I am a powerfully clairsentient person.

The mind within the body

The terms 'gut' feeling or 'gut' intuition are not accidental ones. The area of the body between the heart and the groin which encompasses the stomach and solar plexus is particularly sensitive and could be said to have its own intelligence. Indeed, the stomach and solar plexus contain two of the seven main energy centres or chakras that are integral to the teachings of the Indian Yogic system as discussed in Chapter 4 (see diagram *page* 32). What is more, on a physiological level this region of the body contains a mass of nerve-endings and, while it is quite different, it could be said that it rivals the area of the brain in its complexity. Is it possible that each of us has a brain in our body as well as in our head, and that we have a body-mind or body intelligence to match?

It is in the gut that we tend to experience pleasure and pain; the pleasure of being loved and accepted, perhaps, or the pain of loss or rejection. It is also in the gut that we often experience a feeling for the environment we are in or the people we meet. Walking into a house with an unsettled atmosphere may leave us with an unsettled feeling in the pit of our stomach, while meeting a person who is genuinely kind, honest, friendly and pleased to see us will invariably leave us with a warm glow that is quite tangible.

Your clairsentience supports you in health, happiness and success and guides you to places and people that are most suitable for your well-being. Here is a meditation to help you develop your 'gut' awareness.

Meditation: stimulating 'gut' awareness

Sit comfortably with your back supported and your body open and relaxed, your arms and legs uncrossed. If you prefer you can lie down for this, but make sure that you keep your body open rather than curled up.

To begin, breathe deeply, allowing every breath to fill your lungs completely without straining, and then slowly exhaling. Take a couple of minutes to notice the feeling of your

breath as it moves in and out of your body and then gently allow it to assume its own deep rhythm for a while.

Imagine that the area of your solar plexus (just below the centre of your rib cage) and stomach contains a powerful mind that steadily vibrates with the impulses from its own intelligence, awareness and sensitivity. Every physical sensation, feeling and emotion exists as a ripple of awareness from this extraordinary body-mind.

Imagine yourself breathing directly into your body-mind, the breath from your lungs easily connecting you to your physical and emotional intelligence. As you do this, be aware of stimulating a stronger relationship between this part of yourself and your conscious awareness so that you are always attuned to the power of your gut instinct. What are the feelings that you sense within your body at this time? What are your emotions telling you? Are you feeling calm, excited, sad, joyful, turbulent, peaceful, passionate, angry or loving? Do your best to notice all of your physical and emotional sensations and accept them, allowing them to ebb and flow in their own way and at their own pace.

Next, imagine your solar plexus and stomach filling with coloured light that is reminiscent of bright sunshine. Ripples of clear yellow, vibrant orange, shimmering red and fresh, light gold gently penetrate this area, bringing softness, warmth and illumination. The coloured lights are accompanied by rippling sounds of beautiful chimes and a soft, pulsing heartbeat percussion that creates a greater sense of ease within your body. Breathe deeply and allow yourself to experience a feeling of expansion as your stomach muscles begin to relax and waves of energy spread from there to stimulate and calm every area of your body.

Sense the energy of this light, sound and feeling touching you deeply to awaken the extrasensory power that is available to you through this area of your body. Your 'gut' awareness is healed and stimulated to receive positive sensual information. Your innate clairsentience is strengthened and enhanced. Again, notice any particular feelings or sensations that you receive at this time. Does your body have a message for you? Are there any insights contained within your emotions? Just notice without expectation or judgement and accept what you feel.

When you are ready to complete this exercise, visualize a shield of copper and gold that runs, three hundred and sixty degrees, around your body from just below your heart to just above your groin. Know that you can dissolve this shield whenever you choose to, but that it provides you with solidity, stability, protection and a feeling of security as you continue to expand into greater intuitive awareness.

Clairvoyance

What is clairvoyance?

We often hear people describe psychic ability as clairvoyance. The word 'clairvoyant' is perhaps the term most commonly used to describe anyone with a pronounced psychic ability, and particularly to describe someone who gives psychic readings or 'sittings' on a professional basis. To be more accurate, clairvoyance describes a range of psychic abilities based upon a developed visual sense. The literal meaning of clairvoyance is 'clear sight' or 'clear vision'. A true clairvoyant will receive psychic messages or information through a heightened visual awareness.

A person with developed clairvoyant abilities has a strong sense of inner vision, and is able to receive information in the form of visual images or symbols. Most clairvoyants receive their information internally: some describe having something akin to a cinema screen inside their head with images moving across it; others receive individual symbols that they learn to interpret. Some clairvoyants receive information externally: they are able to see people or animals in spirit, or can observe the subtle energy that circulates around themselves when they walk into a room.

Similar to people with a profound psychic ability in other areas, many clairvoyants will also have a range of other psychic skills (such as clairaudience, clairsentience) but their predominant source of information will tend to be visual. The tendency for all of us, whatever our special skills, is to use our most developed sense first and foremost, while our other senses back up our first impressions and help us to interpret what we perceive.

Subjective clairvoyance

By far the most commonly experienced form of clairvoyance is the ability to receive information internally. Most of us have had the experience of conjuring up an image in our mind's eye when we are remembering a past event or when we are asked to imagine what something we have not seen first-hand looks like. Many clairvoyants receive psychic information in a similar fashion, perceiving visual images, symbols and impressions within their mind's eye which they then interpret accordingly. This ability is sometimes described as 'subjective' clairvoyance.

The third eye

Most subjective clairvoyants receive visual information through what is often described as 'the third eye'. The third eye is one of the seven main chakras or energy centres detailed in the teachings of the Indian Yogic tradition. These chakras are bridges between the physical body and the subtle 'electricity' of the non-physical, esoteric and auric bodies that make up the human energetic system. The third eye or 'brow' chakra is located at the centre of the forehead and is given its name because it is able to receive subtle visual information in an apparently similar manner to the way that the physical eyes receive tangible information from the surrounding environment. The other six main chakras follow the line of the spinal column, and are located at the base of the spine, the abdomen, the solar plexus, the heart, the throat, and the crown (a few inches above the head).

Subjective clairvoyant messages come in the form of the lights, colours, cinematic images or abstract symbols, seen or perceived in the area of the forehead. However, some clairvoyants describe the

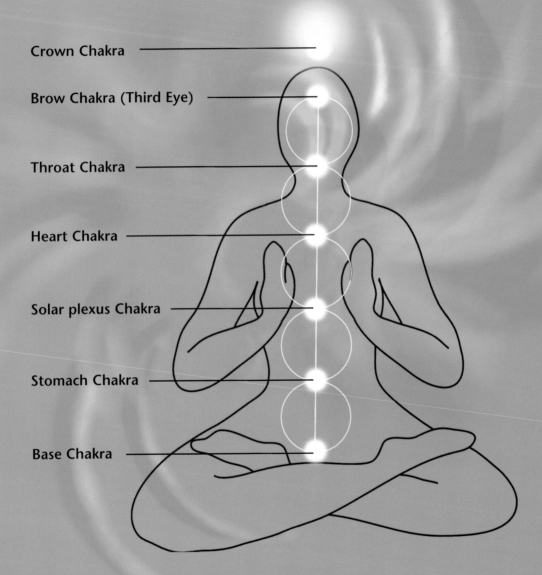

Crown Chakra

Brow Chakra (Third Eye)

Throat Chakra

Heart Chakra

Solar plexus Chakra

Stomach Chakra

Base Chakra

images that they see as being projected forward from their third eye, as if there were a television or cinema screen a few inches in front of their forehead.

Like all psychics, subjective clairvoyants may receive information from their own higher mind or higher awareness, spirit guides, other people (in the form of telepathic communications), environmental influences and numerous other sources we can only theorize about.

Here are some daily declarations and a meditation to help you awaken your higher vision.

Daily declarations for clairvoyant vision:

- It is easy for me to visualize.

- I am willing to receive visual information.

- It is safe and easy for me to open and close my inner eye.

- I easily develop a powerful and effective clairvoyant ability.

- I am willing to receive clairvoyant symbols and messages.

Meditation: opening your inner eye

Sit comfortably with your back supported and your body open and relaxed, your arms and legs uncrossed. If you prefer you can lie down for this, but again make sure that you keep your body open rather than curled up.

To begin, breathe deeply and focus on the area of your third eye in the centre of your forehead. Imagine it as a physical eye, similar to your other eyes below it; visualize it with its eyelid softly closed for peaceful rest and protection. When you are ready, picture your whole forehead area bathed with the gentle golden light of psychic awareness, and then imagine your third eye beginning to open in a way that is similar to a flower opening its petals to the soft morning sunshine.

Notice how clear and beautiful your third eye is. What colour does the pupil of your eye appear to be? If you do not immediately see a colour then make a guess and use your imagination to paint it with your preferred hue. Continue to visualize your eye bathed with a soft golden light and feel it growing stronger, your vision becoming clearer and more perceptive. Hold the idea that your inner eye is completely healthy and is constantly expanding its ability to receive clairvoyant information.

Be aware of any thoughts, feelings and sensations that you have as you do this. Make a mental note of what you see, hear, feel and experience, perhaps writing down any ideas or inspirations once the meditation is complete.

To complete this meditation, bathe your third eye with a light of deep indigo blue to protect it, heal it and keep it safe, then imagine the eyelid softly closing again, cushioning the eye from external influences.

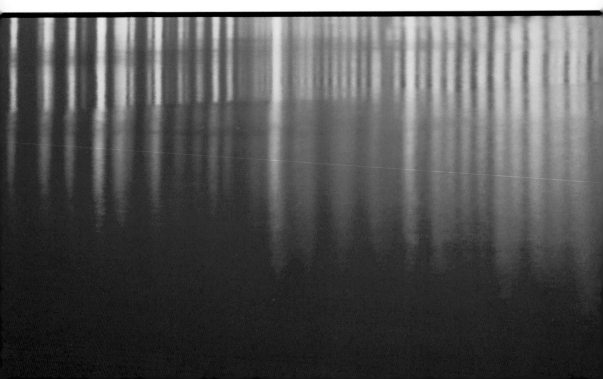

Repeat this exercise on a regular basis, spending some time in a relaxed, receptive, contemplative state to allow for any visual information to be transmitted to you from your higher mind or from some external source. It would be particularly useful to practise this last thing at night, before you go to sleep. Always complete this process in the same way, by bathing the eye with indigo light and closing the eyelid as above.

Interpreting symbols

Many clairvoyants receive psychic information in full or in part, in the form of symbols and abstract images. This kind of clairvoyant work is quite subjective both in its perception of the initial image and in the interpretation of it. However clairvoyants who are practised and experienced at this can be incredibly accurate in their interpretations, and these abstract images can prove to be powerful tools for counselling and guidance.

Clairvoyant images received could relate to past lives, telepathic communication, underlying life goals or life purpose, aspects of healing and overall spiritual development, as well as an individual's current relationships, life choices and career path. Interpretation is something to be learned over time and is not something that is easily taught. There is no clairvoyant symbol that has a set meaning or which can be interpreted using a standard formula. Ultimately we all need to trust ourselves, risk making mistakes and practise as much as we can. Here are some daily declarations to support you.

Daily declarations for effective interpretation:

- It is easy for me to interpret the clairvoyant symbols and images that I receive.

- I am always given the information that I can best understand.

- My powers of interpretation are subtle and effective.

- I interpret everything that I see with care and compassion.

- My vision is blessed with wisdom, imagination and clear understanding.

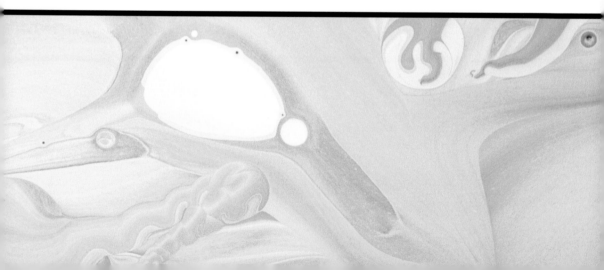

Objective clairvoyance

Objective clairvoyant ability tends to be more unusual than the subjective kind, but there are still many people who have potential within this area, just waiting to be developed. An objective clairvoyant will see objects, animals or people in spirit as if they were physically present. Unlike subjective clairvoyants, who may get a clear picture of similar objects internally, objective clairvoyants see things in the environment around them. In some cases these things can be as three-dimensional as a familiar armchair, although the quality of depth, colour and solidity may vary. The experience is more akin to looking at things through our physical vision rather than through our third eye. However, a level of heightened activity in the brow chakra is usually involved.

Here are some declarations to help you begin.

Daily declarations for objective vision:

- It is safe for me to be an objective clairvoyant.

- I am willing to develop tangible clairvoyant vision.

- My vision is filled with objectivity, solidity, depth and colour.

- I safely stimulate my objective clairvoyant potential.

- It is easy for me to recognize objective clairvoyant images.

Auric Sight

What is auric sight?

The aura is a subtle energetic emanation that surrounds all living things and, as surprising as this may seem to some, surrounds all inanimate objects too. It is often described as being like a subtle electrical or magnetic energy that radiates from human beings, animals, plants, stones, machinery, buildings, household objects and anything else that you can think of.

A person with auric sight will be able to see these subtle emanations. For some, the auric field will appear as a very subtle movement of energy or light around a person or object of focus. This can be a bit like a double or 'ghost' image around figures on a television set when it is not correctly tuned in to the signal. Others will see auras in this way but will also see some subtle colouration within that energy, commonly a silvery blue or grey. People with the most developed auric sight will see a full range of bright, vivid colours.

Auras can vary in texture, quality, feel and colour in relation to the vibrational nature of each individual. We all have a basic vibrational rate that fluctuates from moment to moment as we change and develop.

Sometimes the aura of a human being quite tightly follows the lines and curves of the physical body; at other times it is much more expanded. It can be proportionally larger or smaller in particular areas depending upon an individual person's state of health, energy levels, mood, thought patterns and underlying spiritual purpose.

Developing auric sight

Most people who are willing to practise are able to develop some degree of auric sight, and there are many positive uses for this kind of information. Here are some daily declarations and exercises to help you begin.

Daily declarations for auric vision:

- It is safe for me to see auras.

- I easily see and perceive full-coloured auras.

- I develop a powerful healing relationship with light and colour.

- I effectively and sensitively interpret the colour, density and quality of auras.

- My auric vision brings the benefit of healing for myself and others.

Exercise: Picturing the aura

As before, sit comfortably or lie down with your back supported and your body open and relaxed, your arms and legs uncrossed.

Close your eyes and imagine that you can see an aura around everything. Start with yourself. What might your aura look like at the moment? What colour do you imagine it to be? Is it bright or muted?

How big is it? Is it drawn in fairly close to your body or is it quite large and expanded? Trust your instincts; depending upon how visual you are you may get mental pictures of your aura or you may paint the picture with ideas, concepts, feelings or sensations. Trust your mind to do this in whatever way is natural for you.

Next, open your eyes for a moment and look at an object that is physically close to you. Close your eyes again and imagine its aura. What does it look like? What does it feel like? How is the aura of this object different from your own?

Finally, open your eyes and take a few moments to look more widely at your surroundings. Close your eyes again and imagine that everything around you has an aura. Focus in on specific objects or perhaps a particular plant or a pet and visualize the kind of aura that each object of your focus may have. Trust your inner vision to give you interesting information and make a note of anything that you perceive or imagine. Complete this exercise by opening your eyes and taking a good look around you once again.

Often, beginning to develop auric sight is a matter of simply learning how to re-focus your eyes. Normally our eyes are focused upon the physical nature of solid matter rather than the subtle energetic field within or around it.

Exercise: Re-focusing the eyes

Comfortably hold up one hand a short distance (about 2 ft/50 cm) from your eyes. Look at your hand, noticing the lines, shapes and texture of the skin. Notice the outline of your fingers and thumb as you gently stretch and contract your hand.

Next, leave your fingers loosely apart from one another and then consciously shift your focus from your hand to something in the distance. For instance, if you are indoors you may look beyond your hand to a picture upon the far wall of the room you are sitting in. Allow your hand to remain central to your field of vision but look through it or beyond it towards your distant focus. Practise shifting your vision back and forth a few times between your hand close to you and your chosen object further away. Notice how different your hand looks as you adjust your focus back and forth.

Rest your eyes for a moment and then repeat this process. This time leave your eyes focused in the distance, through or beyond your hand, for a while and notice what you see. Some people may notice a small movement of light or energy around the hand, others may see a double-image etched in white or blue-grey. If you are particularly attuned to auric vision you may see your hand bathed in a field of coloured light.

It does not matter if you see nothing or very little on your first attempts. Just rest your eyes and have another go later. It is enough that you begin to exercise or stretch your vision in this direction. Often it will be easier for you to use your auric vision at certain times of the day. I generally find the soft light of evening particularly good for developing auric ability.

Exercise: The human aura

With a partner, sit opposite each other at a distance of about 3 or 4 ft (90 cm – 1.2 m). Close your eyes for a moment, breathe deeply and imagine that you are gently contacting the subtle energetic field of this person. With your thoughts, ask permission to proceed and request that the auric body of your partner be revealed to you.

Open your eyes and take a good look at your partner physically first, and then, allowing the focus of your eyes to change, look at the aura. It may help for the two of you to synchronize your breathing by inhaling and exhaling at a similar pace and rhythm. Remember to look through, beyond or around the physical image of your friend to see the subtle electrical field that she or he emanates. Notice any clairsentient, clairvoyant or clairaudient information that you also receive as you do this. You may find that your exploration of auric sight stimulates your other psychic channels.

When you complete this exercise remember to separate from your partner by imagining a safety curtain of light, sound and feeling unfurling between you.

Interpreting the aura

If you begin to see coloured auras and wish to interpret what you see, it would be best to start by placing greater emphasis upon the quality of the colour rather than on the colour itself. Ask yourself, 'Is the quality of the aura clear and bright or is it muted or even muddy?', 'What does my intuition tell me about the auric field, does it look strong and well formed or is it wispy, ragged or uneven?', 'Is this the aura of a person who is currently healthy, happy and relaxed or am I receiving different signals?'

The interpretation of auric colours can never be standardized. We are all individuals and therefore each of us has a unique relationship with colour. As a general guide, however, warmer colours relate to slower-moving vibrational energy, physical well-being and material concerns, while cooler colours relate to faster-moving vibrational energy, spiritual well-being and the higher awareness. Here is a simple guide to some of the meanings of different colours. Please use it as a starting point for your intuition and not as a hard-and-fast set of rules.

Red: basic survival
the 'fight or flight' syndrome
physical strength and motivation
material concerns
raw power and energy
anger
revolutionary change

Orange: physical vitality
sensuality
sexuality
pleasure
exercise
creative motivation
warmth
passion

Yellow: inspiration

intellectual activity

the power of the mind

bright ideas

cheerfulness

the bridge between the
mind and the body

the higher intelligence of the body

Green: the natural world

balance

harmony

calmness

love

compassion

ecological awareness

the bridge between the emotions
and higher reason

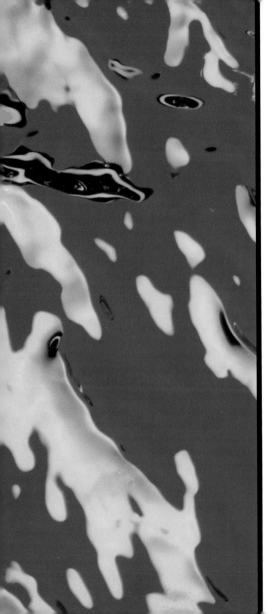

Bright blue: communication
    healing
    teaching ability
    creativity
    expression
    detachment
    inspiration
    the impulse to communicate

Indigo blue: vision
    intuition
    psychic ability
    spiritual protection
    the higher functions
      of the brain
    visual acuity
    auditory skills

Violet: spiritual growth

wisdom

the pathway to enlightenment

the bridge between the mind and
the higher mind

the bridge from the higher mind to
the collective consciousness

Pink: love

warmth

tenderness

the impulse to nurture

childhood concerns

the safety of the inner child

Gold: love
  brilliance
  prosperity
  spiritual radiance
  higher creativity

White: purity
  purification
  the higher realms of perception

Clairaudience

What is clairaudience?

Clairaudience is the term used for psychic hearing abilities. It can be literally defined as 'clear hearing'. A clairaudient person receives psychic information in the form of subtle sounds, words or ideas that are perceived and interpreted through the hearing centres of the brain. Some people report that they hear voices which give them direct information about themselves or about the needs, feelings, actions or motivations of other people. Others do not tangibly 'hear' in this way, they just seem to know things as if they had heard about them.

   Many people have a degree of clairaudience but do not recognize it as such because, like so many other psychic abilities, it has always been there. We may have always received words, thoughts or sounds of inspiration inside our mind without ever questioning their source and their precise nature.

Tuning in to clairaudience

Have you ever heard someone speaking to you only to turn around and realize that there is no one physically present? Like clairvoyance, some clairaudient ability is quite objective in nature. Objective clairaudients hear psychically transmitted sounds and spoken language as if they were hearing them physically.

Most of us, however, are more likely to develop subjective clairaudience. The psychic noises we hear are received as impressions of sounds or words or, alternatively, thoughts, concepts and ideas that just seem to appear in our minds.

Some people receive their best ideas from clairaudient messages. Solutions to

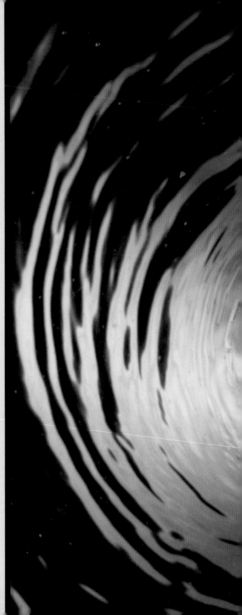

problems, business strategies, new inventions and personal guidance may all be transmitted through clairaudience as well as some of the other psychic senses I have discussed.

Perhaps even more than some other psychic abilities, clairaudience is often a case of 'tuning in' to the right frequencies. Physical sound is said to vibrate at particular rates, and the same is true for clairaudient sound. The key is to widen the range in which we are able to receive and perceive information through the hearing senses so that we are able to discern sound resonance that is outside the confines of our physical sense of hearing. Here are some declarations and exercises to help you begin.

Daily declarations for clairaudience:

- I safely expand the range of my hearing.

- My hearing brings me joy and transformation.

- I open my ears to the sounds of love and laughter.

- It is safe for me to develop my clairaudience.

- My ears are safely attuned to higher frequencies.

Exercise: Tuning the radio

Sit comfortably with your back supported and your body open and relaxed, your arms and legs uncrossed. Breathe deeply and, with your thoughts, place a shield of golden light around your ears for healing and protection. Imagine that the light is filled with a steady, high-pitched sound, a little like a continuous chime that creates a sense of peace, balance and clarity within you. Know that as you expand your range of hearing you automatically tune in to frequencies that are safe and beneficial for you at this time.

Next, imagine yourself with an inner dial like a radio and a knob that you can turn to tune your hearing in to the following frequencies:

1 Your own higher self. Imagine that you are able to tune your hearing in to the frequencies of your own higher awareness. This is the part of you that sees the bigger picture of your life, even when your conscious mind is in a state of confusion. The higher awareness often acts as a bridge for a range of psychic information that originates from outside sources, so it is always a good place to start. You could represent this 'tuning in' to yourself by imagining a subtle change in sound or picturing yourself entering a specific area of your dial.

2 The realms of your higher guides. Hold an intention that you wish to connect only to the realms of higher guidance and ask that you work with guiding energies which truly serve your highest good. Once you have sent out this clear mental message, imagine tuning your hearing to receive clairaudient information from your higher guides. Sense a subtle sound change as before and see yourself moving into another area of your dial.

3 Areas of the natural world. Imagine tuning your hearing so that you are available to the subtle sound vibrations of the natural world. The spirits of animals and plants have their subtle sounds and you may have a special ability to work with nature. Some people can even 'hear' as well as feel changes in the weather before they occur.

In all cases, note any information that comes to you through your ears, your other psychic senses or your imagination. Make a note of any insights you have. You may receive very little clairaudience when you first practise this, but it is worth persisting. After a while you may find that your ears automatically tune in to receive clairaudient information at particular times and in appropriate situations.

Complete this process by bringing your hearing safely back to the frequencies of your own higher awareness and by shielding your ears

once again with protective light and sound. Avoid practising this exercise immediately before you spend time in very busy, noisy places.

Exercise: Listening to guidance

When you have practised 'tuning in' a few times on different occasions you may wish to listen for some specific aspects of guidance. Begin by taking a few minutes to write down some questions or areas of enquiry that are important for you at this time and then 'tune in' in the normal way. Slowly ask your questions and take some time to breathe deeply and listen for responses. Remember to make a note of any insights you receive, and make sure you 'tune out' and protect your hearing once you are complete. Here are some examples of questions you could ask:

'What can I best do at this time to strengthen and enhance my psychic abilities?'

'What can I do to heal my life?'

'How can I best use my psychic gifts?'

In addition, you may wish to ask questions about the source of the information that is coming to you. Whose voice, concept or idea are you listening to? Notice any clairvoyant or clairsentient information that you may also receive.

Words and messages from the higher mind

Most of us certainly receive a degree of clairaudient information from our higher mind. Usually we are unaware of it because it has always been there. Clairaudient words of wisdom may just seem like common sense from a familiar inner voice and, indeed, that is often exactly what it is.

The higher mind or higher awareness gives us many clues or pointers to the life choices we need to make and to the people we need to meet and learn from along the way. We may have words, names or sounds whispered into our ears or particular thoughts or concepts that just seem to arrive in our minds, seemingly from nowhere and sometimes accompanied by interesting sensations around the ears.

Our higher mind is our greatest ally. It has a clearer view of our spiritual development than we have at a conscious level, and it is committed to our greatest purpose, joy and success. It is important to consult this part of ourselves when we are making significant changes in our lives, facing important decisions or wishing to take the appropriate step towards greater psychic awareness.

Daily declarations for higher awareness:

- I trust my own higher wisdom.

- It is safe for me to move to the next level of awareness now.

- I fully connect to the guidance that is available for me.

- I am willing to receive higher guidance.

- I easily receive messages of higher wisdom.

Words of wisdom from guides and helpers

Many psychics believe that they are guided by personalities in spirit who are able to offer valuable information and support through clairaudience, clairvoyance, clairsentience and channelling. Some believe that their guides are people who were once physically alive and who now inhabit a higher spiritual dimension. In some cases, their guides may be considered to be known relatives, friends or former partners who continue to offer guidance to the people they love beyond the limits of their physical mortality. Others, subscribing to a belief in reincarnation, claim the psychic intervention of spirit guides who take the form of personalities they once knew in a former life.

Many more psychics talk of spirits who are considerably more enlightened than we are and who continue to advance their spiritual growth by assisting us with ours. Western spiritualists have claimed guides who, in life, were born of races and cultures that have much to teach us. I have known of healers, channels and clairvoyants who claim to have Chinese doctors, Tibetan monks, African medicine men, native American shamans and Indian mystics as guides. Some consider their spirit guides to be angels: in my opinion, there is a great deal of anecdotal evidence to suggest that true guides are, at least, partly angelic in nature.

Always ask for the highest guidance available to you and do not settle for anything less than loving, considerate, compassionate and balanced psychic information. True spirit guides and angels have our best interests at heart. They come to us with positive intent, good humour, warmth and a genuine concern for our spiritual development.

Telepathy

What is telepathy?

Beloved of science fiction and horror writers, telepathy is often associated with stories about psychic spying, brainwashing and manipulation. The reality is quite different, far less sensational but much more satisfying and, on the whole, quite safe.

Telepathy is an exchange of information directly from the mind of one individual to the mind of another without the need for words to be spoken aloud or any exchange of physical, non-verbal communication such as eye signals, hand gestures or other forms of body language.

We are all telepathic to some degree and go about our daily lives transmitting and receiving information without being consciously aware that we are doing so for much of the time. While we each transmit and receive in different ways, the basic principle is the same: we all act like radios which are able to tune in to information and send out our own signals on certain frequencies. Some of us have a greater ability to receive, others are more able to transmit.

Our individual telepathic abilities are closely linked to our other psychic gifts. If we are more clairvoyant than clairaudient, for instance, then we are much more likely to receive our telepathic information in the form of visual images or symbols than to 'hear' the thoughts of other people in our head.

Telepathic clairsentients may receive a sense of another person's physical or emotional state, even at a distance.

Across great distances

Telepathy can operate at short distances and at great ones. We certainly experience short-distance telepathy on a regular basis with our families and close friends. In these cases, our telepathic abilities become entwined with our other abilities to read and transmit information. For instance, we often know when someone we are close to is angry with us, even when she or he does not express it openly. We may pick up a combination of signals that includes body language, tone of voice, changes in behaviour and clairsentient emotional messages as well as telepathic thoughts that

the person transmits and we receive, loud and clear. In addition, most of us at some time experience having the same idea as our partner, parent, friend or child at exactly the same moment as she or he has it.

   Long-distance telepathy can be just as common as the telepathy we experience at close range, though perhaps it can appear more remarkable because we do not have the more obvious physical signals to rely upon. I regularly think about friends from around the world just as they are writing me a letter or as they are contemplating telephoning me. In fact, even at close range I frequently think about people before they contact me or before I bump into them. Of course, it is not always clear who thought of whom first!

Developing good telepathic communication

Good telepathic communication, when combined with good physical and verbal communication skills, can assist relationships to be harmonious. Very few people are so telepathically developed that they can read another person's mind as easily as picking up a book or playing a tape recording but, at the very least, most of us can develop a telepathic sense of mood and timing. A degree of sensitive telepathy can help to make life a little more peaceful, empathic and compassionate. Here are some declarations to help.

Daily declarations for telepathy:

- I am willing to receive safe and positive telepathic messages.

- The telepathic centres of my mind are fully attuned to higher frequencies.

- I am willing to send telepathic messages of love, positivity and acceptance.

- It is safe for me to be fully telepathic.

- It is easy for me to awaken my innate telepathic abilities.

Channelling and Divination

What is channelling?

The word 'channel' appears to have come from America and covers a broad spectrum of psychic abilities and creative expression. Any of us can be said to be channelling when we lose ourselves in the creative process of painting a picture, writing a book or at any other time when we let go to our creative muse. Some channelling is similar to old-style mediumship, as the channel could be someone who acts as a vehicle for family or friends wishing to communicate from other realms. However, before you get visions of the comic, eccentric mediums found in old movies, let me give you the wider picture.

Healers channel healing energy, acting as a vehicle for healing light. Psychics can channel guidance or information in the form of mental pictures (clairvoyance), hearing subtle sounds or words (clairaudience) and in many other ways. Channelling can be directly spoken, or written in the form of automatic writing. Channels can pass on information from spirit guides and teachers. Some people also channel a form of their own higher mind or higher wisdom. There is really no mystery, we are all capable of learning to channel positive inspirational guidance.

Here are some ways a person can act as a vehicle for information or energy that originates from sources beyond our regular conscious awareness.

Hands-on healing

Hands-on healing has been given many names and is taught and practised using a variety of systems world-wide, but the essential nature of this healing art remains the same. Hands-on healing is the ability to channel a range of spiritual, magnetic or vital energies for the purpose of stimulating the innate self-healing abilities of others. Often these energies are transmitted from one person to another via the hands, hence 'hands-on' healing. A healer may physically place her or his hands upon the head or body of the recipient and allow the energy

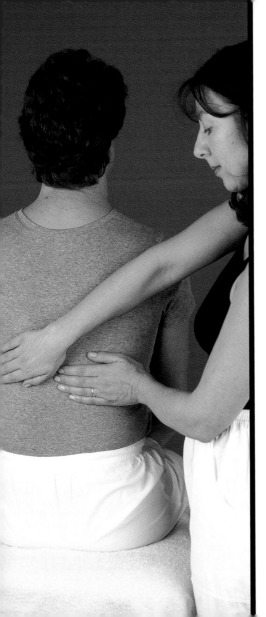

available to flow through him or her and into any area, physical, mental or emotional, that is in need of healing support. However, physical contact is not an essential part of this process, and many healers work by placing their hands near the recipient rather than on her or his body, sending energy through the auric body first, which finds its way to wherever it is needed physically.

The exchange of healing energy can be given by people of all ages and from all social, economic, cultural and religious backgrounds. Similarly, everyone can benefit from healing, regardless of condition, background, or beliefs. You do not even have to be sick to benefit. Many people who are essentially healthy visit healers on a regular basis to help maintain their health and to enhance the quality of their lives.

Some healers do not even get physically close to the people they are helping, but are instead able to channel healing energy from the other side of the room or even from a great distance.

Everyone can learn to give healing. Some people have a highly-developed healing gift, but with practice and a willingness to experiment it is something we can all do.

Direct verbal channelling

The skills of direct verbal channelling are often exactly the same as abilities which have been traditionally described as mediumship. Channels or mediums allow their own personality to temporarily step aside so that the personality of a spirit guide, or guides, can speak directly through them.

Direct verbal channelling entails the use of trance states. The channel relaxes into some degree of trance so that her or his own personality does not get in the way of the information to be transmitted. Many old-style mediums used to work in a state of deep trance, and some still do. A deep trance can be described as going into a state of deep sleep, remaining conscious at some level but being generally unaware of the specific information that is coming through or of the time that is elapsing.

More common than deep trance work is the practice of assuming a light trance for the purposes of channelling. Some light trance states can be quite similar to deep trance in that the channel may still assume a depth of relaxation or become disconnected from normal waking reality, but a degree of conscious awareness remains. While there is a greater risk of the information becoming distorted by the personality of the channel, this does allow for a healthy balance of inspired guidance and rational thought.

It is important to remember that the information received is to be acted upon with discernment rather than automatically accepted at face value. With this in mind you will probably derive great benefit from channelling sessions.

Automatic writing

Automatic writing is similar to direct verbal channelling except that it makes use of the hand you write with rather than your voice for channelled guidance. I have seen pieces of writing that give general advice for spiritual development as well as texts that serve to communicate personal information from someone in spirit to a relative or friend who is still physically alive. The other purpose of automatic writing is to give the spirit guides a vehicle through which to produce a piece of creative work.

During automatic writing, channels hold a pen in their hands or sit in front of a computer keyboard and, in a similar manner to verbal channelling, allow their personality to step aside temporarily. Rather than attempting to control the flow of written or typed information, they do their best to allow their hands to operate the pen or the keyboard spontaneously. Their conscious will, if fully engaged, would only wish to control the nature of the information and manipulate the text into a form that would make immediate sense to the rational mind. With the conscious will relaxed, the higher will or the will of spirit guides can direct the flow of information.

Some examples of free-hand automatic writing I have seen appeared to be so loosely controlled at first glance that the individual words and

letters were a challenge to identify. However, on closer examination clearer patterns began to emerge and words, phrases or whole sentences started to build a profound picture of the nature of the communication. With practice, early attempts at automatic writing can be superseded by written language that displays a clear purpose or narrative.

The psychic artist

Some channels specialize in co-creating channelled artwork. They allow their hands to be used for the painting, drawing or sculpture of channelled images and forms. I have met psychic artists who work with people by drawing their friends or relatives in spirit or by channelling images of spirit guides onto paper or canvas.

There are other channels who knowingly or unconsciously collaborate on pieces of

original artwork. Some pyschic artists have claimed contact with great masters who have taught them special skills or, using them as a vehicle, have continued to add new works of art to collections they produced while still alive.

Some psychic art is also sacred art. Many shamanic or healing traditions from around the world have traditionally included the use of sacred art in ceremonies of healing and as a bridge between the physical and non-physical worlds. For instance, the Navajo people, who now chiefly reside in the southwestern region of the United States, have practices of sand painting that have been passed down from generation to generation.

The uses of divination

The practices of divination play an important part in the development of psychic skills and in the purpose and delivery of channelled information.

Traditionally, many shamans, healers, mystics and medicine people were skilled in the arts of divination. Depending upon their specific cultural origins they would often use divination tools such as bones, runes, tarot cards, the I Ching or astrological charts to assist those who sought their advice or counsel. Whatever methodology was employed, practices of this kind would allow the shaman to combine her or his natural counselling, healing and psychic abilities in the service of others.

Today many good astrologers, diviners and card readers are also skilled psychics who use their craft as a focus for their visionary or intuitive abilities. The process of laying a spread of tarot cards, for instance, gives a card reader a certain amount of basic information about a client's current emotional, mental and spiritual state. This information provides a reader with a framework that can be built upon using their unique psychic and intuitive awareness. The present and future trends that may be indicated to anyone with a good working knowledge of the cards can be used as the basis for a degree of predictive psychic reading that can help others to make positive and constructive choices about their lives.

Tarot and other divination systems have the additional advantage of providing both the reader and the client with a strong visual or sensual component that speaks directly to the subconscious mind in ways that are more powerful and perhaps more direct than words alone. This helps everyone involved to externalize thoughts, feelings, needs, desires and aspects of intuitive awareness which might otherwise remain suppressed or untapped. Most sets of tarot cards bear images that represent powerful human and spiritual archetypes; rune stones are tactile as well as bearing a small degree of visual information; the chart wheel employed by Western astrologers serves both as a valuable technical guide to interpretation and as a 'mandala' or visual focus for the intuition.

Utilized positively and with an intention to empower others, divination tools can provide us with an excellent focus for our counselling skills and psychic ablities.

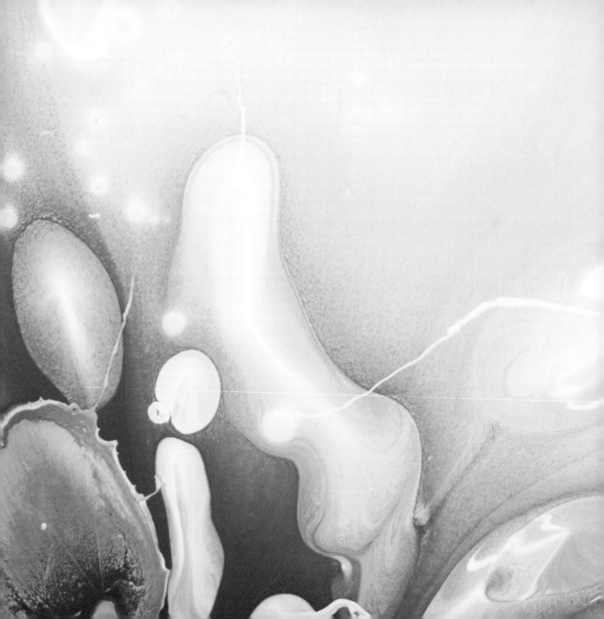

Divination as an aid to psychic development

The use of divination tools in itself can stimulate psychic and intuitive development. As an ongoing exercise, choose one or two systems of divination to work with over a period of time. While you are learning, you may initially choose to consult the cards, stone tablets or astrological charts purely for your own guidance; after a short time you will probably find that many friends or family members will also take an interest in what you are doing and ask you to read for them.

When you begin to read for others it is fine to let them know that you are just learning and ask for their help and support as you begin to practise. After a while you will probably find that your psychic abilities automatically fill the spaces between the pieces of textbook information that you have learned, allowing your readings to become more rounded and mature. Remember to be as positive, constructive and helpful as possible and, as always, trust your intuition.

Continuing the Psychic Tradition

There are many unwritten histories of people throughout the ages who have had a degree of developed psychic ability and who have used this ability to serve the higher good of others as well as to help direct the course of their own lives as effectively as possible. Psychics and healers have been given many different names within many different cultural traditions, from high priest and priestess to visionary, seer, medicine man, medicine woman, diviner, oracle, witch and shaman.

As you embark upon the next stage of your psychic development it is good to know that we live in a time when many cultures are once again learning to value natural intuitive abilities and healing skills. Indeed, psychics and healers are beginning to work hand in hand with medical doctors, therapists, scientists, spiritual ministers and the business community to facilitate many benefits for all concerned. I am confident that if you handle your unique psychic potential with love and positive intentions then your abilities will blossom. Your psychic potential will stimulate your spiritual growth and have a positive knock-on effect on all areas of your life and relationships.

The following meditation and declarations are intended to help strengthen your connection to your higher purpose.

Meditation: connecting to your inner purpose

Before going to sleep and first thing when you wake up, imagine yourself being bathed in the light of your higher purpose.

Within your imagination give this light a beautiful colour, sound and fragrance appropriate for your well-being and spiritual development at this time. Visualize the light of your higher purpose washing through you every moment of the day and night. Picture it, in advance, touching everyone you will have contact with during the day ahead, generating feelings of love and ease within all of your relationships. See the light opening up and creating wonderful opportunities for you, illuminating your pathway to future happiness and success.

Repeat this meditation on a regular basis, always holding an intention that you are connecting to the highest guidance available to you for your own greatest good and the greatest good of all concerned.

Daily declarations for spiritual mastery:

- I am my own healer, spiritual teacher and guide.

- I am a spiritual being on a human path.

- My life is always guided and inspired.

- My psychic abilities always stimulate my spiritual growth.

- My life is filled with love and purpose.